F A T H E R

Thank You for...

THANK YOU
FOR BEING
THE ONE WHO LISTENED.

THANKS

FOR HELPING M

EE MY TRUE SELF.

Dad, you knew who I really was when you said

_____

_____

_____

_____

_____

_____

_____

*T*HANKS

FOR BEING MY

ROCK OF GIBRALTAR.

We will always remember where we were when this happened

_____

_____

_____

_____

_____

_____

_____

_____

*Y*OUR LOVE MEANS EVERYTHING TO ME.

FOR YOU, DAD.

Thanks for being a role model to me when it came to

_____

_____

_____

_____

_____

_____

_____

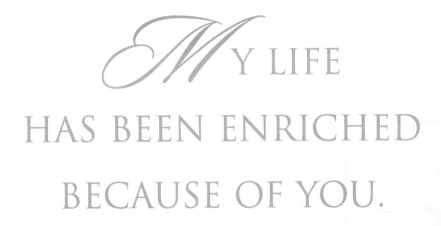

$\mathcal{M}$Y LIFE

HAS BEEN ENRICHED

BECAUSE OF YOU.

THANK YOU

FOR YOU

ENEROSITY.

When I needed it most, you gave me

_____

_____

_____

_____

_____

_____

_____

THANK YOU
FOR LOVING ME
DAY IN AND DAY OUT.

YOU

WERE A GOO

ROVIDER FOR OUR FAMILY.

Thanks for providing us with

_____

_____

_____

_____

_____

_____

_____

_____

THANK YOU
FOR ALWAYS
FINDING A WAY
TO WORK THINGS OUT.

YOU
HAD FAITH I

ME, DAD.

Thanks for building me up when I

_____

_____

_____

_____

_____

_____

_____

_____

*Y*OUR WISDOM
HAS STAYED.

THANKS
FOR HELPIN

E STAY THE COURSE.

I will never forget

_____

_____

_____

_____

_____

_____

_____

_____

THANK YOU
FOR NOT
JUDGING ME.

OF *You*.

Thanks for showing me the many ways to make this happen

_____

_____

_____

_____

_____

_____

_____

I LOVE YOU, DAD.

DREAMS
ARE IMPORTAN

N LIFE.

Thank you for listening to mine

_____

_____

_____

_____

_____

_____

_____

_____

THANK YOU
FOR THE INFLUENCE
YOU'VE HAD ON MY LIFE.

Here are a few kind words you offered me at just the right time

_____

_____

_____

_____

_____

_____

_____

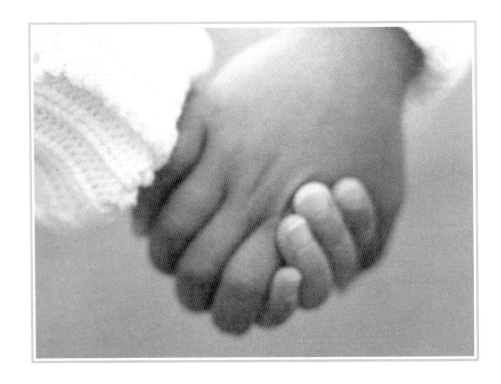

I AM GRATEFUL
FOR YOUR COMFORT.

TIME.

TIME.

You have always entertained me with

_____

_____

_____

_____

_____

_____

_____

THANK YOU
FOR BEING THE BEST
THAT YOU COULD BE.

Thanks

FOR SHOWING ME WHA

T MEANS TO ENJOY LIFE.

I remember your loving advice when I

_____

_____

_____

_____

_____

_____

_____

_____

THANK YOU
FOR PREPARING ME
FOR LIFE.

My HEART

IS FULL O

HANKS.

I will never forget this gift from you

_____

_____

_____

_____

_____

_____

_____

*T*HANKS FOR
TELLING ME THE TRUTH
WHEN I NEEDED
TO HEAR IT.

YOU

HAVE SHARE

Thanks for telling me stories like this one

_____

_____

_____

_____

_____

_____

_____

_____

THANK YOU
FOR LETTING ME SHAR

I am forever grateful for this memory

_____

_____

_____

_____

_____

_____

_____

_____

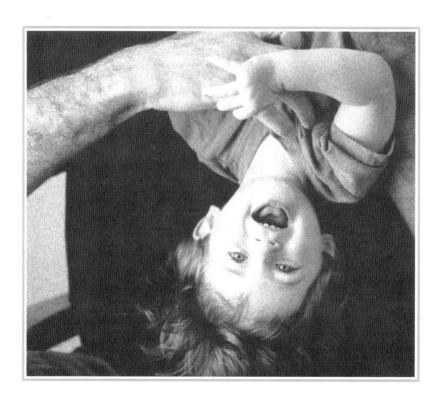

THANK YOU
FOR THE MEMORIES.

© 2004 Havoc Publishing
San Diego, California
U.S.A.

Text by Maureen Webster

ISBN 0-7416-1317-4

www.havocpub.com

Made in Korea